What readers are saying about *In 30 Minutes®*

Excel Basi(

"Fas   )e. The
mate   ⌐ccessible
with :   ⌐ne more like a friend
or co-wo⌐   ⌐xcel than a technical manual."

"**An excellent little guide**. For those who already know their way around Excel, it'll be a good refresher course. For those who don't, it's a clear, easy-to-follow handbook of time-saving and stress-avoiding skills in Excel. Definitely plan on passing it around the office."

Dropbox In 30 Minutes

"I was intimidated by the whole idea of storing my files in the cloud, but **this book took me through the process and made it so easy**."

"**This was truly a 30-minute tutorial** and I have mastered the basics without bugging my 20-year-old son! Yahoo!"

"**Very engaging and witty**."

LinkedIn In 30 Minutes

"**This book does everything it claims**. It gives you a great introduction to LinkedIn and gives you tips on how to make a good profile."

"I already had a LinkedIn account, which I use on a regular basis, but still found the book very helpful. The author gave examples and explained why it is important to detail and promote your account. **Reading this book has motivated me to return to my account** and update it to make it more thorough and attention-grabbing."

Google Drive & Docs In 30 Minutes

"I bought your Google Docs guide myself (my new company uses it) and it was really handy. **I loved it**."

"I have been impressed by the writing style and how easy it was to get very familiar and start leveraging Google Docs. **I can't wait for more titles**. Nice job!"

Learn more about *In 30 Minutes*® guides at in30minutes.com

LinkedIn In 30 Minutes

How to create a rock-solid profile and build connections that matter

By Melanie Pinola

Contents

Introduction: Why You Should Be Using LinkedIn: 1
Ways You Can Use LinkedIn: **2**
What's in This Guide: **4**

Chapter 1 - Make a Killer LinkedIn Profile: 6
Create an Account on LinkedIn: **6**
The LinkedIn Profile: Your Career Showcase: **9**
The Key to Making the Most of LinkedIn: **11**
Strategy #1: Match Your Profile with Your Goals: **12**
Strategy #2: Use Search-Friendly Keywords Throughout
Your Profile: **13**
Strategy #3: Aim for a 100% Complete Profile: **14**
Create a Compelling LinkedIn Profile: **15**
Section 1: Headline, Photo, and URL: **16**
Section 2: Background: **19**
Other Sections: Activity, Recommendations, Connections,
Groups, Following: **27**
Make Your Profile Public: **28**
Summary: Your LinkedIn Profile Checklist: **28**

Chapter 2 - Become a LinkedIn Networking Pro: 30
The Three Degrees of Separation on LinkedIn: **30**
Match Your Connection Strategy with
Your Goals: **32**
How to Find People to Connect With: **34**
Invite People from Your Email Address Book: **34**
See People You Might Know Related to Your Profile: **36**
Why Not Use The Default Invitations? **37**
Find More Connections by Searching: **38**
Connect to People Outside of Your Network with InMail: **40**
Get Introduced: **41**
Join LinkedIn Groups: **43**
How You Can Interact with Your LinkedIn Connections: **45**

Send a Message to Your Connections: **45**
Add Recommendations or Endorse Skills: **46**
Share Status Updates: **47**
Summary: Top Tips for Building Your LinkedIn Network: **49**

Chapter 3 - How to Use LinkedIn to Find and Land a Job: 50
Tweak Your Profile to Complement Your Job Search: **50**
3 Things Your LinkedIn Profile Must Communicate: **51**
How to Address Gaps and other Special Job Seeker
Situations: **54**
How to Find and Apply to Job Listings on LinkedIn: **56**
View Recommended Jobs: **56**
How to Use LinkedIn's Job Search: **57**
How to Apply to Jobs on LinkedIn: **60**
How to Access the Hidden Job Market on LinkedIn: **60**
How to Network on LinkedIn When You Need a Job: **61**
Find Job Opportunities Posted By Your Contacts: **59**
A LinkedIn Job-Searching Strategy: **62**

Chapter 4 - How to Use LinkedIn to Advance Your Career: 64
How Using LinkedIn Can Enhance
Your Career: **64**
Stay Current in Your Industry: **65**
News on LinkedIn: **65**
Find Out What Others Are Talking About on LinkedIn: **67**
Maintain Relationships and Find People Who Can Help You:
67

Chapter 5 - LinkedIn Power User Tips and Tricks: 69
How to Send a Message to (Almost) Anyone on LinkedIn for
Free: **69**
Organize Your LinkedIn Connections: **70**
View Contact History and Stay Connected with LinkedIn
Contacts: **71**
Organize Your Connections with Custom Tags: **72**

Tweak Your LinkedIn Privacy Settings: **73**
LinkedIn Premium and Job Seeker Premium: **75**
Job Seeker Premium: **76**
LinkedIn Premium: **76**

A Personal Message From The Author, And A Request: **78**
About the Author: **79**
Credits: **80**
Bonus: Introduction To *Twitter In 30 Minutes*: **81**
Bonus: Introduction To *Google Drive & Docs In 30 Minutes*: **88**
More *In 30 Minutes* Guides: **92**

Introduction: Why You Should Be Using LinkedIn

If you're serious about taking your career to the next level, you need to be on LinkedIn. In the past five years, the online career network has opened doors for millions of people, transforming the way they market themselves and enabling them to vastly expand their professional networks. In addition, companies are using LinkedIn to recruit everyone from entry-level employees to CEOs. In the next 30 minutes, this guide will show you how to best present yourself on LinkedIn and leverage other features that will help advance your career.

LinkedIn is the world's largest professional network, with more than 200 million members and counting. Hiring managers and headhunters actively use LinkedIn. Companies big and small, and millions of professionals — including executives from every Fortune 500 company — use it. You need to actively use it, too. The reason is simple: **There's no better social networking tool (or other online tool, for that matter) for furthering your career than LinkedIn.**

That's a bold statement, but research backs it up. Consider this:

- 98% of recruiters used social media to find talent in 2012, according to a Bullhorn survey. Guess which network they used to place job candidates? That's right — LinkedIn. Some 93% of the surveyed staffing professionals placed candidates through LinkedIn, compared to just 17% for Facebook and 13% for Twitter.

- Another Bullhorn survey of over 77,500 recruiters found that 48% of them post jobs on LinkedIn *and nowhere else on social media.*

- 90% of surveyed LinkedIn users said they thought the site is useful because:

    - "It helps me to connect to individuals in my industry as possible clients"

    - "It is more professional than Facebook"

    - "It allows me to hire people that I wouldn't regularly meet"

Ways You Can Use LinkedIn

Although many people think of LinkedIn mostly as a tool for job seekers, you can benefit substantially from using LinkedIn even if you're not ready to leave your current job. **Think of the site as a free online résumé, industry insights tool, and digital Rolodex rolled into one**.

Here are a few ways people are using LinkedIn to achieve their career goals:

- **Dan is an IT professional who's satisfied with his current job** … but he wouldn't say "no" if a more attractive opportunity presented itself! He doesn't actively check job boards, but he set up his LinkedIn profile so headhunters can easily find him.

- **Gabe is the owner of a small accounting firm**. He uses LinkedIn to promote his services to potential and current clients, discuss business strategies and general accounting topics with other LinkedIn members, and keep up with his competitors' developments.

- **Dana is a recent college graduate** who just got her first job doing graphic design. She uses LinkedIn to share — and discover —

interesting information about her field, help her grow her expertise and build her professional reputation.

- **Mike has been out of work for over a year**, after layoffs at the manufacturing company where he used to work. LinkedIn helps him update and modernize his résumé, find companies currently hiring for his skills, and connect with previous colleagues, employers, and classmates who could help him re-enter the workforce.

- **April is a mid-level marketing manager** who's been at the same company for the last 10 years with little advancement — and she's ready to move up! She uses LinkedIn to find relevant job openings, research and follow companies she's interested in, and find people in her network who could help with her job search.

Although these people are in different stages of their careers and use LinkedIn for different purposes, they have two things in common: They're interested in maintaining or advancing their careers, and LinkedIn is central to their career development strategies. Facebook might be great for socializing and Twitter for keeping abreast of the news (or following celebrities), but LinkedIn is for your livelihood.

Note also that even though LinkedIn once targeted people working in technology-related industries and white-collar professionals, the network has since expanded to every occupation and industry. You can be a chef, a cardiologist, or a carpenter, yet still build a network and find other ways to leverage LinkedIn.

What's in This Guide

Whether you're completely new to LinkedIn or have already set up an account but are left thinking "What now?", this guide is for you. In just 30 minutes, you'll learn the basics of getting started with LinkedIn, such as how to:

- Create a strong LinkedIn profile (Chapter 1)

- Build and grow your professional network (Chapter 2)

- Use LinkedIn to find a job, stay current in your industry, and advance your career (Chapters 3 and 4)

- Make even better use of LinkedIn with power user tricks such as organizing your LinkedIn contacts and changing privacy settings (Chapter 5, and online at linkedin.in30minutes.com)

At the end of each chapter is a convenient checklist, which will help ensure that you have hit the most important steps.

By the way, if you're the type of person who cringes when someone gushes about "networking," don't worry. As a shy, card-carrying introvert, "networking" is not my favorite word either. One of the great things about LinkedIn is this isn't the same kind of networking that happens at conventions, where you're wearing a name tag, trying to meet strangers, and awkwardly attempting to make small talk. **LinkedIn is networking without the pressure**. Using the service, you can reach out to people you know — *and those they know* — virtually. In fact, people expect to be contacted, and others might also reach out to you. That's what the site is for!

Ready to get started? Now's a great time to find a copy of your most recently updated résumé and fire up your browser...

Chapter 1

Make a Killer LinkedIn Profile

Now that you know some of the benefits of using LinkedIn, you're probably itching to put the service to use so it can open career doors for *you*. The first step is to create your free LinkedIn account, which takes less than two minutes. After that, we'll set up your LinkedIn profile, which you can think of as your own personal branding page on the network and the Internet as a whole. Even if you've already set up your LinkedIn profile, you won't want to miss some of the tips in this chapter for making your profile more effective (and maybe even irresistible!).

Create an Account on LinkedIn

Joining LinkedIn couldn't be easier: Just visit LinkedIn.com to register for a free account. A setup wizard will walk you through the steps. While LinkedIn also offers premium subscriptions, the free account is more than enough for most users' needs (paid accounts are discussed in more detail in Chapter 5: Power User Tips and Tricks.)

Here's what the free, basic account registration form looks like:

Get started – it's free.

Registration takes less than 2 minutes.

First name	Last name

Email address

Password (6 or more characters)

Join now

As you can see, all you need to enter is your name, email address, and your desired password to get started. Two tips, though, before you hit that "Join Now" button:

- **Choose the best email address**: If you have multiple email addresses, use the one most business associates have for you on file. That way, people who know your work will more easily find you on the network. Don't worry about being locked into your work email address. Later on, you can add additional email addresses to your account. If you leave your current company, you can always change the primary email address used for your LinkedIn account.

- **Select a strong password**: LinkedIn requires a minimum of six characters for your password, but for the highest security, you should choose a very long, complex password that isn't used for any other site. Your password, which can be as long as 41 characters, should be a mix of capital and lowercase letters, numbers, and symbols.

After clicking the button to join LinkedIn, you'll then be asked to enter your location and current job status. Depending on whether you select "Employed", "Job seeker", or "Student" for your status, LinkedIn will ask you for additional details, such as company name and industry or school name. You can also select "Self-employed" as your status.

M, let's start creating your professional profile

* Country	United States
* ZIP Code	
	e.g. 94043
I am currently:	◉ Employed ○ Job Seeker ○ Student
* Job title	
	☐ I am self-employed
* Company	

Create my profile

Don't worry too much about what you enter here. Just fill in the basic information. We're going to tweak it later (in the next section) to be focused toward your goals.

The next step of the wizard asks you to connect your email address to LinkedIn to find people you know on the service. Skip this step for now by clicking the "Skip this step" link at the bottom of the form. Don't worry, we'll come back to it later. The reason for the delay: We want to tailor your profile before sharing it with the world!

Finally, in the last screen, click the link to have a confirmation email sent to your inbox so you can activate your account. In the email LinkedIn sends you, click on the confirmation link and then you'll be ready to build your professional identity on LinkedIn.

The LinkedIn Profile: Your Career Showcase

When recruiters, co-workers, old classmates, and other people Google your name and click on a link to you on LinkedIn, your profile page is what they will see. They'll learn about your work history, education, skills, interests, reputation, and other details you provide. It's like your own "Who's Who" entry on LinkedIn.

Here's a condensed version of my profile, showing each main section. Key information appears at the top of the profile, including a photo, location, the number of connections, and a summary:

Melanie Pinola

Freelance Writer I Specializing in Technology, Personal Finance, Telework, and "Life hacking"

Greater New York City Area | Writing and Editing

Current   Self-Employed, About.com
Previous   Ensemble Media, handshake Marketing
Education   Harvard University Extension School

Improve your profile | Edit Profile ▾ | 500+ connections

in www.linkedin.com/in/melaniepinola/ | 📇 Contact Info

Activity

Share an update...

Background

🔍 **Summary**

I'm a freelance writer with over twelve years of experience in content development for both the web and traditional media. I have a passion for finding useful information and compelling stories—and the best way to present them to readers. Whether it's a concise blog post or an in-depth feature article, I'll wrestle with a word or paragraph until it's just right for the intended audience. (In fact, I've rewritten this paragraph a dozen times just to tell you that.)

Further down are sections for work experience, endorsements from other people, and educational background:

In the LinkedIn template, you can easily add other sections, including volunteer experience, awards, and more. We'll go through each section in the step-by-step walkthrough below.

The Key to Making the Most of LinkedIn

First, though, it's **crucial to understand what separates an average LinkedIn profile from those that truly stand out**. Many people make the mistake of breezing through LinkedIn's simple wizards to create the most barebones online profile. They then walk away, only to later wonder why LinkedIn "doesn't work" for them. Although you can add as little information to your profile as you want, **the more you customize your page, the better**

your chances of LinkedIn actually being a useful tool (instead of something that's there just for the heck of it, like a stack of business cards you never hand out.)

To make your profile as effective as possible, we'll use a three-prong strategy:

1. **Align your profile with your goals** (so you attract the right kinds of opportunities)

2. **Incorporate search-friendly keywords** to highlight your skills and strengths (this will make it easier for people to find you on the network)

3. **Create as complete a profile as possible** (so anyone who reads your profile will know what you're all about)

Strategy #1: Match Your Profile with Your Goals

How do you want the world to see you professionally? What kinds of work do you enjoy doing? Why are you on LinkedIn? Those are the questions you should think about when creating your LinkedIn profile, so it's aligned with your personal brand. While marketing-speak like "personal brand" feels fake to many of us, we're really just talking about setting the right tone for your profile and positioning yourself for the kinds of opportunities you're interested in.

For example, you might be a consultant ready to take on bigger clients. Therefore, you want to be seen as an expert who can handle the most demanding projects. Or, you could be a job seeker looking to advance into a management role. In this situation, it's important to stress your leadership skills. Maybe you don't even know what you want to do with your career yet, but know that it's a good idea to connect with other professionals. Whatever your situation, **take a minute to identify what you would like LinkedIn to do for you and whom you want to be seen as**.

(In addition to the tips and instructions in this chapter, in Chapter 3, I'll show you additional strategies for customizing your profile specifically if you're job hunting.)

Strategy #2: Use Search-Friendly Keywords Throughout Your Profile

When recruiters and companies look for people on LinkedIn, they do so using LinkedIn's search features. To find the right match for an open position, they enter keywords into the search field that correspond to certain skills or experiences. Examples include "social media strategist," "MySQL database design," "CNC machinist," and "inventory control manager." If you fail to include the keywords that highlight your own skills or strengths, no one will find you on LinkedIn when they search for those keywords. With over 200 million members on LinkedIn, just showing up in relevant search results is vital.

These keywords are also essential because they influence how you're found *outside* of LinkedIn. Search engines like Google prioritize the keywords in your profile (particularly the headline) when placing you in search results and rankings.

So before you start creating your profile (we're getting there soon, don't worry!), you'll save a lot of time and aggravation if you **write down the 3 to 5 keywords related to your skills and the job you currently have or want**

to have. If you've pulled out your résumé after you first started reading this guide, the document should contain plenty of keywords to choose from. Look for phrases that define your areas of expertise, job roles and responsibilities, or your other unique selling points.

You can also look at job listings for your occupation (on sites such as Indeed and Monster.com, for example) to find relevant keywords employers are using. Copy and paste descriptions from ideal job postings into a site like wordle.net to see the most prominent words in the listings — those would make great keywords for your profile. You'll use this keyword list later to help fill in key areas of your profile, including your headline and summary.

> **INSIDER TIP**: If you were a recruiter looking for someone like yourself, what keywords would you enter in the search box? Those are the keywords that can make your profile more visible and enticing to others.
>
> (Warning: Beware of using keywords like "ninja," "guru" and any word ending in "-fu". Unless you truly are a Kung-fu master, these terms are not the best keywords to use in your profile for search optimization.)

Strategy #3: Aim for a 100% Complete Profile

When you view your profile, LinkedIn will show you a "profile strength meter" that shows you how complete your profile is. Don't ignore it. Filling out your profile as much as possible will help you rank at the top in search results and give you a leg up on your job competition. LinkedIn members who have complete profiles are 40 times more likely to be viewed and receive opportunities through the network, according to LinkedIn's research. To get to 100% completion, your profile needs to include:

- A profile photo

- Your industry and location

- A summary about yourself

- At least two past positions with descriptions of your roles

- A minimum of five skills

- Where you went to school

- At least 50 connections

With your goals and keywords in mind, let's fill out all of these areas and get your profile up and running.

Create a Compelling LinkedIn Profile

Creating your profile can take as little as 10 minutes, or take much longer, depending on how much you tweak it. However, you can update your profile as often as you like, so feel free to take your time and work on your profile in stages or come back to polish it whenever you want. **Your profile is a living, breathing portrait of you and your work.**

> **INSIDER TIP**: If you're already connected to people on LinkedIn and are editing your profile, turn off Activity Broadcasts so people don't get multiple, annoying emails every time you update a sentence in your profile. This is especially important if you don't want your boss to know you're looking for another job. Click on your profile photo in

the top navigation bar, then go to Privacy & Settings, and click "Turn on/off your activity broadcasts" under the Privacy Controls section to be more clandestine about beefing up your profile.

Also, if you're just starting out and not ready to share your profile or have others see your work in progress, turn off your public profile. Click on your profile photo in the top navigation bar, then Privacy & Settings, and in the Profile section click the "Edit your public profile" link. In the next page, change the setting in the "Customize Your Public Profile" in the box at right to "Make my public profile visible to no one."

Now let's get started on building your LinkedIn profile. Click on "Profile" in the main menu, then "Edit profile." Every detail on your profile can be edited by clicking on the icon that looks like a pencil. Let's go in order:

Section 1: Headline, Photo, and URL

The most prominent part of your profile is the section at the very top of the page containing your photo, name, headline, location, industry, and contact information. Yes, this is just your basic information, but don't let that deceive you. What you add to this virtual calling card can make a big difference on whether people who land on your profile will continue reading or not. This is your chance to make a good first impression.

Photo: Unlike other social networks like Facebook and Twitter, the quality of your photo really matters here. One of the biggest profile mistakes is to use an inappropriate or poor-quality photo, such as a blurry, five-year-old photo of you with your dog. If possible, get your photo professionally taken. At the very least, choose a recent headshot that you actually like and that radiates your warmth, approachability, and trustworthiness (or whatever qualities you want to project).

Above all, don't neglect to include a photo. If you don't upload a photo to LinkedIn, you'll be seen as just a generic gray outline in the space that usually holds a photo. This is a dead giveaway you don't actually use the network (and don't care to).

Further, people who see a profile that does not include a photo will be less likely to read more about that person. Profiles with photos are *seven times* more likely to be viewed than those without one, according to LinkedIn.

Your photo can be a JPG, GIF, or PNG file up to 4MB in file size. Upload a photo at least as large as 500 by 500 pixels; that way, people can click on the photo thumbnail to get a larger and clearer view of you if they wish. Don't worry about the photo orientation (square, landscape, or portrait); after you upload the photo, you'll be able to crop the photo to your liking.

> **INSIDER TIP**: Use the background in your profile photo to emphasize what you do. While your profile photo should focus on you and not have any distracting elements in the background, if done right, the photo background could subtly support your career interests by placing you in context. For example, you could have a blur of trees behind you if you're a forester or a football stadium if you're a sports writer.

Your name: This one's easy: Just enter the name you use professionally. If you have a maiden name and want people to find you by that, you can click the "Former Name" link to include it as well.

Headline: LinkedIn automatically populates the headline (the blurb under your name) with your current title and company, but should not leave it at that. You can expand it, or create something completely different.

Consider these two headlines:

1. Default LinkedIn headline, based on current job: *"Senior Product Manager at Zoomjax"*

2. Custom headline, created by the profile owner: *"Senior Product Manager at Zoomjax | Expert Team Builder | Developer of Scalable, Targeted Ad Platforms for Media Buyers"*

The second headline, by adding just a few more keywords, gives a better picture of this person and his capabilities. This is extremely important, because when your profile comes up in search, only your name, headline, location, and industry are shown. **Your headline is what will convince the searcher to look at your profile**. It's a 120-character hook that should tell people what you do — and why they should care.

Add your most relevant keywords here (as discussed in the section above), separated with a comma or the "|" symbol (found above the Enter key on the keyboard) or other symbol.

For example, here are a couple of headlines that stand out from the typical "Title at Company" formula:

Todd Wheatland 1st
Author, Speaker | Content Marketing, Social Media, HR, Employer Branding, SlideShare | VP Marketing @ Kelly Services
Paris Area, France · Management Consulting

Tom Spring 1st
Executive Editor & Senior Technology Writer: 20 years of experience creating award-winning stories and features
Greater Boston Area · Publishing

Depending on your goals, you could also create a catchy and personable type of tagline, such as:

Myk Klemmë 1st
Marketing Consultant & UX/UI Architect: I translate geek speak to business speak.
San Francisco Bay Area · Marketing and Advertising

Paul Philleo 1st
Game Industry Swiss Army Knife
San Francisco Bay Area · Writing and Editing
▸ **2 shared connections** · Similar · 👥 **500+**

Note that the headlines above, while different from each other, all offer potential employers and collaborators a short, clear explanation of the value offered by each of the professionals.

URL: The other important part to edit in this section is your LinkedIn URL, found just under your photo. This is the link to your public profile page. By default, LinkedIn gives you a URL with numbers appended to it, such as www.linkedin.com/in/mpinola/1/395/648. Click the edit link to make this address, also called a "vanity URL," more memorable, easier to share, and search-friendly by ditching the numbers and using your full name: e.g., www.linkedin.com/in/melaniepinola. If your URL name is taken, you can do a variation, such as mpinola, or one of the suggestions LinkedIn will offer you.

Section 2: Background

The background section is where your résumé comes in handy, since this is where you highlight your experience, accomplishments, and skills, much like you would on a paper résumé. Your background section shouldn't be an exact duplicate of your résumé, however. **Think of it as the place to tell your professional story and position yourself for your career goals**.

The three main parts of the background are the summary, experience, and education. Here's how to tackle them.

Summary: The summary section is a snapshot of your career. Like a good book introduction, the summary should draw people in — or at least help them quickly understand what you're all about: What you do, what you know, what you're looking for, and how you can help them. Basically, this is where you "sell yourself" in 200 to 300 words.

Be honest as you describe your background, but also don't be shy about your accomplishments. This is where you showcase your strengths and sprinkle (as naturally as you can) all of those perfect keywords you came up with earlier that will make you stand out in search.

> **INSIDER TIP**: As you write this section, think about the unique features of your career that you want prospective employers, colleagues, and others to know. What are your proudest accomplishments? How did you get to where you are now? What are you passionate about? If you can quantify your achievements, all the better (answer the "how" question: how long you did something, how many things you produced, how much you surpassed goals, etc.)

Here are a couple of examples of targeted, effective summaries:

LinkedIn CEO Jeff Weiner's summary highlights his previous achievements and main areas of expertise (edited for brevity below):

Internet executive with over 17 years of experience, including general management of mid to large size organizations, corporate development, product development, business operations, and strategy.

Currently CEO at LinkedIn, the web's largest and most powerful network of professionals.

Prior to LinkedIn, was an Executive in Residence at Accel Partners and Greylock Partners. Primarily focused on advising the leadership teams of the firm's existing consumer technology portfolio companies while also working closely with the firm's partners to evaluate new investment opportunities.

Specialties:general management, corporate development, product development, business operations, strategy, product marketing, non-profit governance.

Intel program manager Jeff Hodgkinson uses headings to make his summary easy to read and lists numerous reputation-building details (edited for brevity below):

WHO I AM:

Project/Program Management Professional with over 31 years experience and success in Fortune 100 enterprise level Project/ Program Management.

WHAT I HAVE DONE:

- *Delivered results for numerous and diverse high profile*

programs and projects in varying complexity.

• *Mentored 100's of Project/Program Managers in obtaining various certifications and credentials.*

• *Authored / co-authored articles in various PM publications, e-newsletters, websites, & blogs.*

WHAT I ENJOY AS A SIDE INTEREST:

• *Evangelizing the cost benefits of solar power and thermal*

• *Promoting global interest in 'Green' and sustainability Project Management*

• *Residential energy efficiency initiatives with my HELP 'Home Energy Lowering Program'*

WHAT ARE MY EXPERIENCE AREAS:

• *Agile Project Mgmt*

• *Business Networking*

• *Coaching/Mentoring*

• *Contract Management/Negotiation*

• *Energy Efficiency/Solar*

And content specialist Wendy Brache knows a thing or two about good content:

I specialize in content strategy and development.

If you're reading this, you understand the value of content. And, of course, you know it's not too hard to dump a bunch of general material out there on the interwebs. What's more difficult is delivering interesting, easily digestible, tailored content to a segmented audience to accomplish a specific goal.

Here's what good content is all about: that beautiful little sliver in the Venn diagram that contains both "what your customers care about" + "what you do differently than the competition."

I work with clients to build a great story and segment-specific messaging that reaches the right person at the right time in the right way.

As with your headline and other parts of LinkedIn, **how you craft your profile summary should be all about your goals for using the network**. Two to three paragraphs are usually enough to get your point across. However, the length depends again on your intended audience. You might craft your summary with a bulleted list of your accomplishments so it's easy for recruiters to scan, or write a more in-depth story-like summary to help your connections really get to know you. If you need more inspiration, do a search for people in a similar position and industry as yourself and see how they've created their profiles.

After those introductory paragraphs, list your specialties (which could be your previous titles, skills, industry categories, and other keywords) either separated by commas or as a bulleted list. For example:

"Specialties: marketing, integrated marketing, consumer market research, branding, strategic partnerships."

This will pack in those search-friendly terms at the top of your profile.

At the bottom of your summary, add what marketers and advertisers call a "call to action." If you're open to new opportunities or want to be contacted, let everyone know this at the end and how you can be reached (e.g., email, phone, or a visit to your blog).

Experience: After your short summary, it's time to dig into your work experience. Although you might be tempted to copy and paste your résumé word-for-word into the experience section, resist that urge. Ideally, your résumé is a targeted document that you send to a company to prove your value for a specific position, using keywords from the job description and demonstrating your value in previous related jobs. Your LinkedIn profile, on the other hand, can be richer and reach a broader audience than just one hiring manager at a specific company. **It should be a supplement to your résumé, rather than an online duplicate.**

What should you include in the experience section? As with résumés, you'll need to provide a title, company, and work dates. These should match your résumé timeline exactly. However, in the details section you can communicate your strengths and passions, as well as what makes you unique. You can also be less formal if you want to, and leave out overused phrases like "results-oriented team-player" and "excellent interpersonal skills."

To make your profile 100% complete, you'll need to list at least two work experiences. You can include volunteer work, internships, and any freelancing or side business experience here.

Consider this example from Troy D. White, Director of Marketing and

Membership for Future Business Leaders of America (FBLA-PBL), who details his capabilities and accomplishments (edited for brevity):

> *FBLA-PBL is an education association that helps students prepare for careers in business and business-related fields. With over 250,000 members, it is the largest student business organization in the world.*
>
> *As a member of the Senior Leadership Team, I lead all activities that significantly increase and retain membership and enhance membership benefits, including developing and disseminating core branding and communications messages; optimizing multiple channels — print and digital — using analytics and data; generating publicity, articles and public outreach; and working collaboratively with internal departments and statewide organizations to increase conference attendance and implement new educational programs.*
>
> *Key accomplishments:*
>
> - *Spearheaded new "Innovation Center," a public idea generation community. Led team that evaluates and implements ideas*
>
> - *Increased revenues 3% while decreasing expenses 15%, yielding ROI of 34%*

Note how he briefly introduces the organization he works for, summarizes his activities (lots of keywords!), and lists his work highlights in an easy-to-scan bulleted list.

In short, tell the story of your work history as descriptively and as thoroughly as you like, based on your goals.

Education: Adding a school in the education area will not only help your profile be 100% complete, it also can help you connect with former or fellow classmates on LinkedIn. The only required field is the name of the school, but you can add dates (including your expected graduation date, if you're currently studying), degree, field of study, grade, activities and societies (e.g., Alpha Phi Omega), and other details in the description (e.g., scholarships or student travel). Any kind of education or training can be added here, not just those from colleges or universities.

Skills and Expertise: Finally, the last part of your background that's required for a complete profile is a list of at least five skills. These are keywords that describe your areas of expertise. Just start typing in the box and LinkedIn will recommend available keywords that match, as shown below:

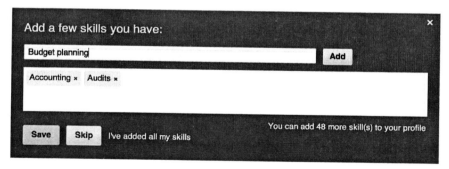

Other background sections: Though not required for a 100% complete profile, other template sections that can be added to your background include:

- Languages

- Volunteer Experience & Causes

- Honors & Awards

- Organizations

- Projects

- Publications

- Additional Info (Interests, Personal Details like birthday and marital status)

You don't have to add any of these, but if they help you tell a better story or stand out from the crowd, go ahead and add them. It's as easy as clicking the "+" sign and filling in the form.

Other Sections: Activity, Recommendations, Connections, Groups, Following

Besides your basic information and background sections, your LinkedIn profile may also contain sections that reveal your activity on the network:

- Status updates you share with your network

- Recommendations others write for you on LinkedIn

- A list of members you're connected to

- The LinkedIn groups you've joined

- The companies and people you're "following" and get updates from.

These are pulled in automatically by LinkedIn, but you can customize what's shown in these sections by clicking the pencil icon to edit these sections.

Make Your Profile Public

With your profile completed and set just the way you want, now you can make it public and start sharing it with the world. If you currently have your public profile set to hidden, click on your profile photo in the navigation bar, then Privacy & Settings, and click the "Edit your public profile" link. In the "Customize Your Public Profile" box at right, you can specify which content areas are shown on your public LinkedIn profile page.

Summary: Your LinkedIn Profile Checklist

In this section, you learned how to set up your LinkedIn profile so it showcases your unique professional experience and skills. Here's a list of things you shouldn't forget:

- If setting up a new account, don't connect to people (or have your email scanned for connections) before you set up your profile. If you're editing an existing profile (or looking for a new job and don't want your boss to know about it), turn off activity broadcasts. Remember to turn them back on when you're ready to share.

- Figure out your goals and the keywords most relevant to your professional identity before creating your profile.

- Aim for a 100% complete profile.

- Make sure your photo puts you in the best light (a professional photograph is ideal).

- Create a headline that summarizes what you do and what makes you unique.

- Customize your profile URL with your name.

- When adding a website to your profile, choose "Other" for the category so you can add a descriptive name for the link instead of LinkedIn's default "Website" name.

- Showcase your strengths in your summary and experience sections. Focus on answering "What do I want people who see my profile to know most about my work and capabilities?" and "show, don't tell" by answering *how* you've excelled in your work.

- Include keywords as naturally as possible throughout your profile.

- Use your résumé to identify key highlights to add to your profile, but don't just copy your résumé verbatim. Try to have your personality show through here.

- Add extra sections (education, honors & awards, projects, etc.) to tell the right story about your professional development and capabilities and help you stand out. Don't be shy!

Now that you have a professional online presence on LinkedIn, it's time to find who you know on the network. The power of LinkedIn is really in the connections, which just happens to be the subject of the next chapter.

Chapter 2

Become a LinkedIn Networking Pro

You've probably heard this old saying before: "It's not *what* you know, it's *who* you know." Well, on LinkedIn, both what you know *and* who you know can make a huge difference for your career prospects. In the previous chapter, we fine-tuned your LinkedIn profile to highlight your skills, strengths, and experience — the "what" that companies and others want to know about you. The "who" side comes from your connections on LinkedIn. It's not just who you directly know — it's also who your contacts know and, even further out, who *they* know.

LinkedIn is a powerful tool because it turns a small number of connections into a huge, professional network — one that's far more vast and diverse than you could build with real-life schmoozing. Workers of all kinds, from executives to those new to the job market, in every industry and over 200 countries, are gathered in one place — and chances are you can be somehow connected to them. With the 600 or so people I'm directly connected to on LinkedIn, for example, I'm linked to over 11 *million* professionals on the network and can reach out to them for help or information. Below, I'll show you how easy it is to start building your valuable network.

The Three Degrees of Separation on LinkedIn

LinkedIn works on the same principle as the "six degrees of separation" theory (also known as the "six degrees of Kevin Bacon"), which says everyone is just six introductions away from any other person in the world.

LinkedIn connects you to people within three degrees:

- 1st degree connections are those you connect with directly. These are the co-workers, friends, colleagues, and others you send an invitation to connect with and who accept your invitation, or they send you an invitation that you accept.

- 2nd degree connections are all the people who directly connect with your 1st degree connections (but you aren't directly connected to). In other words, the "friends of friends".

- 3rd degree connections are the people directly connected to your 2nd degree connections

In LinkedIn lingo, your "connections" are your 1st degree connections, those you link up with with via invitations to join each other's networks. You can freely send messages to these people via LinkedIn.

Your entire LinkedIn "network," however, also includes the 2nd degree and 3rd degree connections, as well as fellow LinkedIn group members (more on that in a bit). These are people you can send an invitation to become 1st degree connections or get introduced to on LinkedIn — but cannot contact directly through a free LinkedIn message. (We'll talk more about ways to communicate with LinkedIn members later in this chapter.)

Put in Kevin Bacon terms:

- Kevin Bacon and fellow actor Mickey Jones were in a 1991 movie called *Pyrates* together. Since they know each other, Mickey Jones is a first-degree connection for Kevin Bacon.

- Mickey Jones was in the movie *Tin Cup* with golfer Phil Mickelson, who doesn't know Kevin Bacon directly. Phil Mickelson is therefore a second-degree connection for Bacon.

- Phil Mickelson knows Tiger Woods, who is not otherwise connected to either Jones or Bacon. Tiger Woods is a third-degree connection for Mr. Bacon.

This is the beauty of LinkedIn: Kevin Bacon could ask Mickey Jones to introduce him to Phil Mickelson, and then get introduced by Mickelson to Tiger Woods — and they can all get together for a nice round of golf. LinkedIn, similarly, can connect you to professionals you might not otherwise meet or know — people who could be an inside connection at a company, a source of knowledge, or someone you could help.

Match Your Connection Strategy with Your Goals

At the risk of sounding like a broken record, your goals for using LinkedIn should direct how you use the service — and that includes whom you connect with on LinkedIn and how you build those relationships.

There are a couple of ways you can go about this:

Only connect with people you know well or want to know: This is the strategy that makes sense for most people. By limiting your connections to those you are close to, your LinkedIn network will consist of only quality connections — people who are more likely to care about helping you and who can vouch for your work. LinkedIn recommends having at least 50 connections for a 100% complete profile, but as you'll see below, there are many places you can find quality connections.

Connect with as many people as possible: Some people take a more open networking approach, willing to connect with anyone on the network. There are groups on LinkedIn for open networkers (called LIONs, for LinkedIn Open Networkers), where you can find lists of people who accept all invitations to connect. Whether you become an official LION or you just decide to connect to as many people as possible (maybe even people you barely know), there's one tremendous benefit to this strategy: Your network will grow exponentially. This links you to far, far more people who might be able to help you professionally.

There are downsides to the open network approach as well. Having so many connections can muddy up your LinkedIn feeds (what's shared to you in the homepage and elsewhere) and make it hard to find the contacts that truly matter. It takes more work managing a large network (imagine having hundreds of thousands of contacts in your email address book!), and it's harder to build deep relationships and separate the spam from the useful messages.

A broad connection strategy might make sense for anyone who has to promote a product or service, whether you're a consultant, public relations professional, or anyone else whose job involves doling out a lot of business cards to strangers in real life.

If you're the kind of person who is more likely to talk to just a few select people, though, rather than work a whole room, then open networking online probably isn't for you. Still, it pays to connect to as many people you do know, because **the larger your network is, the better your chances of having a connection for your goals**.

Whichever strategy you choose, let's start with finding the connections that already exist in your life.

How to Find People to Connect With

LinkedIn makes it dead simple to find possible connections and invite them to join your network. In fact, there are a number of ways to go about it. The steps below might take you five to ten minutes each (depending on your number of contacts), but they're well worth it.

Invite People from Your Email Address Book

You can have LinkedIn comb Gmail, Outlook, Yahoo! Mail, Hotmail, AOL, or any of your email addresses for contacts to add as connections on LinkedIn. This is the fastest method for sending invitations en masse to your contacts.

However, sending mass invitations via email has a serious limitation: You can't customize the email that goes out to each person. It's often better to personalize the invitation email, so unless you're in a huge hurry, don't send out mass invitations. Instead, you can add connections by using one of the other methods outlined later in this chapter.

If you do decide to send bulk invites, here are the steps involved:

1. Click on the icon of a gray avatar with a plus sign on it (to the left of your profile photo).

2. Then click on either the "Add Connections" link or select one of the email icons available (Gmail, Yahoo, Hotmail, or Other).

3. Enter your email address and click "Continue".

4. You'll be asked to log into your email account to allow LinkedIn to access your address book.

5. After connecting LinkedIn with your email account, LinkedIn will then show you a list of people from your address book who are LinkedIn members. By default, all of these contacts are selected, so if you hit the "Add Connection(s)" button, you'll send an invite to all of them. The invite says "I'd like to invite you to my professional network" and cannot be changed. Uncheck the ones you don't want to invite. Alternatively, click the "Skip this step" link at the bottom to continue without inviting anyone on this list.

6. On the next screen, you can send an invitation to all of the contacts who aren't on LinkedIn yet. Again, deselect the ones you don't want to send a message to or click "Skip this step" to exit.

See Who You Already Know on LinkedIn

Get started by adding your email address.

Your email

Continue

🔒 **Your contacts are safe with us!**
We'll import your address book to suggest connections and help you manage your contacts. And we won't store your password or email anyone without your permission.
Learn More

Another option is to import contacts from a file (.csv, .txt., or .vcf), which you can create from an email application such as Outlook or Apple Mail. Click on the "Any Email" button shown in the screenshot above and then click the

"Upload contacts file" to choose the file to import.

See People You Might Know Related to Your Profile

After searching your email contacts via the steps above, LinkedIn will offer a button to see more people you may know. This will take you to a grid of people from various companies and schools related to your profile. (If you don't go through the wizard above, you can find this link in your profile. Click Profile > View Profile and in the right sidebar, scroll down until you see the heading "People You May Know," which is under the Profile Strength meter. Click on the "People You May Know" text to get to this screen.)

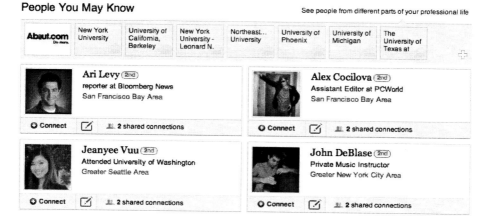

You can filter the list by clicking on one of the organization/school boxes at the top of the grid.

For each person, you can simply click the "Connect" button to send an invitation with the default "I'd like to add you to my professional network" message. Better yet, click the icon that looks like a pen in a box. Doing so will let you create a personal invitation. I highly recommend writing personal invitations, which can dramatically increase the chance of the recipients accepting the connection with you.

Why Not Use The Default Invitations?

Be careful when you send an automated invitation request, especially if the contact might not remember you very well. If someone you invite rejects your invitation and clicks the "I don't know this person" button, LinkedIn will start tracking those "IDK" responses. LinkedIn has been known to restrict accounts that get to five IDKs, so they can no longer send new invitations without entering the recipients' email addresses. Avoid this risk by only inviting people who will likely want to connect to you (or at least won't say "Who the heck is this stranger?"). Personalizing your connection invitation will make a big difference.

For example, let's say you met someone at a convention and traded business cards, but it's been a few months since the event. The person may no longer remember you. If you want to add this person to your LinkedIn network, compose a brief note (300 characters maximum) that will jog his or her memory instead of using the default LinkedIn invitation. For example:

> *"Hi Bob, Great meeting you at the Food & Drinks Expo last week. Thanks for introducing me to your company's distribution services. I hope the wine buyers' survey was useful. I'd like to add you to my LinkedIn network. Please let me know if I can be of further help. Thanks, Sam Smith, CA Organic Wines"*

In your personalized note, incorporate why you reached out, how you can help (or help each other), and foster the kind of mutually beneficial professional connection LinkedIn was designed for. By taking the time and effort to personalize your invitation (for example, by commenting on a common interest you saw in the other person's profile), you'll sound more like someone who truly wants to connect on LinkedIn, rather than someone who's robo-inviting every familiar name.

Find More Connections by Searching

You don't have to stop at just your email address book and the "people you might know" suggestions from LinkedIn. You can also search for possible connections by name, company, school, or industry. Just enter what you're looking for in the search box in the navigation bar and press the Enter key for a list of results, which you can filter down by current company, location, industry, school, and more. For example, if you were looking for "Joe Smith", here is what would turn up at the top of the search results for People:

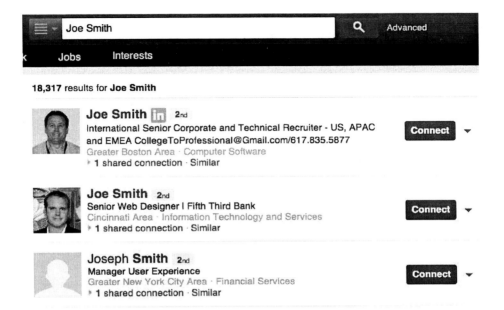

You can also find possible connections you didn't know existed. The LinkedIn search results will point out members who have shared connections with you or are in a group you've joined (LinkedIn groups are described more fully below).

Once you've found the person you want to invite into your network, click on the Connect button to send an invitation request. LinkedIn will ask you to specify how you know this person. For example, if you choose "Colleague" or "We've done business together," you will get a drop-down box to select the company from your profile that matches. Any selection except for "I don't know Joe" will get your invitation sent to the person. However, note that if you choose "Other" for how you know Joe, you'll have to put in Joe's email address to verify you really know him. Remember to personalize your invitation!

✉ Invite **Joe** to connect on LinkedIn

How do you know Joe?

○ Colleague
○ Classmate
○ We've done business together
○ Friend
○ Other
○ I don't know Joe

Include a personal note: (optional)

I'd like to add you to my professional network on LinkedIn.

- Melanie Pinola

Important: Only invite people you know well and who know you. Find out why.

[Send Invitation] or Cancel

After your contact accepts your invitation, he or she will be in your network and you can freely send messages to each other on LinkedIn, share status updates, and more.

Connect to People Outside of Your Network with InMail

Some people won't have a Connect button next to their names. Instead, you'll see an option to "Send an InMail." Unlike the free messages you can send to any of your direct connections, InMails are paid messages.

You'll see the InMail button instead of the Connect button when:

- LinkedIn members have made their profiles more private and not open to public networking requests. Their last names are displayed as just an initial (e.g., Kevin B.).

- The LinkedIn member isn't a first-degree connection, someone you invited to join your network or who invited you.

To send a message to one of these people, LinkedIn wants you to buy an InMail message. Each InMail costs $10. You can purchase 1 InMail at a time, or lots of 3, 5, or 10 InMails. The InMail messages are guaranteed in a sense that if you don't get a response in seven days, you can use that InMail credit to connect with someone else. If you have a paid LinkedIn account, you get more InMail messages to send.

If you really need to contact someone who's outside of your network, an InMail will help you do that. However, in Chapter 5, Power User Tips, I'll show you a secret workaround to contacting nearly anyone on LinkedIn without buying InMail credits. For now, let's continue on the official route.

Get Introduced

As with the Kevin Bacon and Tiger Woods example in the previous chapter, you can also ask your connections to introduce you to other LinkedIn members they know. This is better than sending a direct invitation if the person doesn't know you. (It's like matchmaking in real life: "Hey Gustavo, I know you're friends with Julia. Can you hook me up?" Except this is platonic, professional matchmaking.)

For example, I don't know President Barack Obama personally. If I search for him on LinkedIn, however, I see we have a few shared connections. Clicking on that shared connections link, LinkedIn tells me which of my direct connections (including LIONs who connect with *everyone*) have a first-degree connection with the president. If I want to add Obama as a first-degree connection, I could ask one of these people for an introduction.

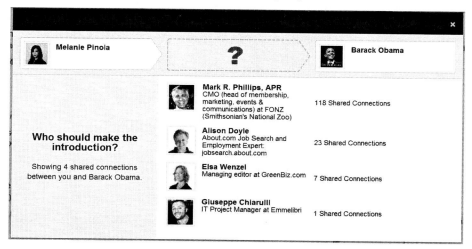

You can also see shared connections from any profile page. Look at the sidebar on the right for a "How You're Connected" section, which includes a "Get Introduced" link.

To ask for an introduction, click on the name of the person most likely to help you out and compose your request. For the best chance of success, make your introduction request personalized and to the point. Be aware that your contact could forward or share the introduction request with the person you want to link up with, so professionalism is key. For example:

> "Hi Mark, I'm currently working on a project that could help alleviate our nation's unemployment crisis and would like to share our preliminary results with influential government leaders. I see that you're connected on LinkedIn to President Obama. Would you be willing to introduce me to him? Thanks for considering my request, and don't hesitate to reach out if I can help you in the future as well."

Obviously, you can use this to try to connect to anyone your contacts know, not just the president of the United States. For example, someone I "linked up with" on LinkedIn had a direct connection to a person I wanted to interview who was outside of my networking circles. A quick message on LinkedIn to that "connector" person was all it took to get us in contact.

Join LinkedIn Groups

LinkedIn groups are forums dedicated to specific interests or kinds of people, such as University of California alumni, state government employees, or anyone working in the cable industry. Groups are also the easiest way to vastly increase the number of people in your network, since other group members are part of your network (like 3rd-degree connections).

By joining and participating in LinkedIn groups, you can also find job openings, discover the "hot topics" group members are most interested in, and contribute to stimulating discussions. In general, the more you give in group discussions, the more you may get out of it. (To be honest, though, not all groups are useful. Some are just loaded with spam and self-promotion posts. If you find you're not getting much value from a particular group, look for better-managed ones.)

There are several ways to find groups that might suit your interests and career aspirations. You could use LinkedIn's search function (e.g., by industry, location, or interests) or investigate the groups your connections belong to. You can also let LinkedIn suggest some groups for you:

1. Click on "Interests" then "Groups" in the navigation bar.

2. Below any groups you've already joined, LinkedIn highlights a few

"Groups you might be interested in." Click on one to find out more or click the Join button.

3. For a larger list of groups you might want to join, search for a related word and then in the search results click on "Groups" in the left navigation menu.

Here are some of the top results in LinkedIn groups for the search term "Books":

I already belong to the first group, so I am shown the option to post something to it, such as a question or a link. Below that is the Books and Writers group, to which I do not belong. Clicking the Join button will submit an application to join the group (requests are reviewed by the group's moderators). The third group is dedicated to children's books. I can view the contents, and also have the option of joining it.

How You Can Interact with Your LinkedIn Connections

Connecting to people on LinkedIn isn't about collecting contacts. It's about, well, actually *connecting* with them, specifically in a career-oriented way (and sometimes in a social way!).

Besides viewing your connections' profiles and seeing their status updates on your LinkedIn homepage, you'll also be able to send messages through the service and interact with them in other ways.

Send a Message to Your Connections

You can send a message to people in your network through their profile pages, from your Inbox, or from your My Connections page.

- **From the Inbox**: Click on the email icon in the top navigation bar. Then, in the black "Messages" heading, click on the compose message icon, which looks like a square with a pen on it. This is the fastest way to get to the message composition screen.

- **From My Connections**: Click on "Contacts" in the navigation bar, then "Connections." Here, you can filter your connections list or search for a contact. Click on the checkbox next to the name or names of people you want to write a message to. This is convenient when you want to send messages to multiple people on LinkedIn at once.

- **From your connection's profile**: Click on the "Send a message" button right beneath your contact's summary on the profile page.

When you send a message through LinkedIn, it will be delivered via email (the name will say something like "Joe Smith via LinkedIn" on the email) and the recipient will also get a notification in LinkedIn.

Add Recommendations or Endorse Skills

One unwritten rule of using LinkedIn is you should both give and take on the service. Two ways to "give" on the networking site are to offer a recommendation for your contacts and endorse their skills. Since these can be posted to your connections' profile pages, validating or verifying their expertise, it's a much-appreciated act.

How are recommendations and endorsements different?

Recommendations are comments that can be a sentence or several paragraphs long. If your connection chooses to accept the recommendation, it'll be added to his or her profile under the relevant background section. Profiles with recommendations get an extra boost during job searches.

Endorsements, on the other hand, are the speediest way to vouch for someone's areas of expertise: You just click on the skills the person has listed in his or her profile, and then your name (along with others who also endorse that person's skills) gets added alongside the skill keyword. For example:

11	Mobile Applications	
11	Web Content	
10	Content Strategy	
9	Entrepreneurship	

You can ask one of your contacts to recommend *you*, by going to Profile in the navigation bar, then Edit Profile. Scroll down to the Recommendations section, click on the pencil icon, and then on the right click the "Ask to be recommended" link. In the next window, fill out the form to send a recommendation request from a contact.

Share Status Updates

Finally, you can interact with your connections on LinkedIn through the status update box on the homepage of your profile. You can regularly add important news, links to online articles, quick tips, whatever you're currently reading, and more. It's a great way to stay connected with everyone in your network, even those you're not regularly in touch with outside of LinkedIn.

How it works:

- Type in what you want to share in 600 characters or less.

- If you add a website link, LinkedIn will pull in a summary of the information below your text.

- If you want to grab a particular person's attention, type in his or her name with the + sign before it (e.g., "+Melanie Pinola") along with what you're sharing.

- In the "Share with:" drop-down box, you can limit who can see your status updates (all of LinkedIn or just your connections.)

- If you have a Twitter account linked to the service, you can also have your update posted to Twitter. (Note: If you also share your LinkedIn updates on Twitter, try to limit your update to 140 characters.)

- Your status update will appear in the activity section at the top of your profile as well as when your connections visit the front page of LinkedIn.com while logged in..

Here's what this looks like:

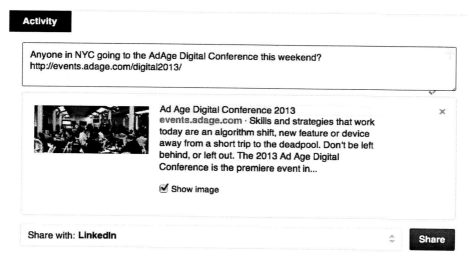

Others on LinkedIn can comment on your updates, and you can (and should) comment on your connections' updates.

Summary: Top Tips for Building Your LinkedIn Network

- Send a personalized invitation rather than the generic default one whenever you can.

- Be careful who you invite to join your network. Too many "I Don't Know This Person" responses could land you in LinkedIn jail.

- Join LinkedIn groups to vastly expand your network. Also, be sure to follow your groups' rules.

- Stay active and connected on LinkedIn by sharing status updates, recommending or endorsing your connections, commenting on your connections' updates, and jumping into the conversations in a few different groups.

- Regularly look for connection opportunities, since the network is rapidly growing (to the tune of two new members every second).

- Keep updates and messages professional, polite, and useful (i.e., not just self-promotional. We all know that kind of pest!). Focus on the mutual benefits of your connection, rather than what you want from the other person.

- Connect on the online network the way you would in your real professional life: with authenticity, a desire to be helpful, and your own personality showing through.

In the next chapter, we'll explore how to network on LinkedIn for specific purposes, such as finding — and landing — a job.

Chapter 3

How to Use LinkedIn to Find and Land a Job

Congratulations! Once you've completed the steps in the last two chapters, you'll be a huge step ahead of others with little or no presence on LinkedIn. With your completed profile and expanding professional network, you're now more easily found on LinkedIn, and have a greater ability to reach and interact with millions of other members.

You're also now better positioned to tap into the power of LinkedIn to support your specific career goals, such as getting a job or advancing in your career. In this chapter, I'll show you how to use LinkedIn to land your next job (if you're not looking to leave your company, move on to Chapter 4, which focuses on enhancing your current career).

Tweak Your Profile to Complement Your Job Search

In a study commissioned by Microsoft, 86% of employers said that a positive online reputation influences their hiring decisions, while 70% have rejected candidates because of negative information about them online.

A well-crafted LinkedIn profile can be central to establishing a positive online reputation. Your LinkedIn profile, which we set up for completeness in Chapter 1, not only gives you control of your online reputation, it also shows potential employers that you're adept at using social media and web apps such as LinkedIn. Let's further target and beef up your profile with your job search in mind.

3 Things Your LinkedIn Profile Must Communicate

Your LinkedIn profile should leave no room for doubt about the kind of job you're looking for and why you're the best person for that position. Create a strong, focused profile with these three tips:

1. Your LinkedIn profile must be consistent with how you portray yourself elsewhere. Not only should your official résumé match the experience you list on LinkedIn, but it also should be consistent with Twitter and public Facebook information. For instance, if dates of employment in previous years don't match up, or your LinkedIn profile indicates you live in a different part of the country than what your Twitter profile says, that can be confusing to recruiters and even raise some red flags.

2. Your LinkedIn profile must include keywords for specific skills that match your desired job. I talked about the importance of keywords in Chapter 1, but it's absolutely crucial to fine-tune them when you're job hunting. This will require a little detective work. Search job listings on LinkedIn, and for each one that looks appealing to you, identify the keywords that come up frequently, particularly in the "Desired Skills & Experience" section. For example, a job listing for a Medical Billing and Coding Manager lists these desired skills:

Desired Skills & Experience

Certified Professional Coding Certificate (preferable)
Billing and Coding supervisory experience in a physician organization/medical practice.
Managed Care Insurance coding experience
Electronic Medical Records (EClinical Works preferred)
Thorough knowledge of CPT, ICD-9 coding, medical compliance, HIPPA, credentialing, enrollment, claim formatting issues that cause payment errors, and medical insurance follow up
Computer proficiency, specifically Excel and Windows
Strong organization and communication skills in order to interact effectively with others in the medical field
Self-motivated to deliver results

So, if you were to apply for a job such as this, you could optimize your profile by including the relevant keywords, such as "certified professional coding certificate," "coding," "medical insurance," and so on.

Also look for role models (people who are successful in the exact job you want) on LinkedIn, by searching on job titles and reading members' profiles. Focus again on the words repeated often and the skills most frequently listed. Joan Bastek ranks near the top in my search results for "medical billing and coding" because these terms are listed multiple times in her profile:

Medical Billing and Coding
Physician's Resources, Ltd.
October 2010 – August 2012 (1 year 11 months)

Medical Billing, Customer Service, contacting insurance companies for outstanding payment of claims.

Accounts Receivable
Global Vision
November 2009 – September 2010 (11 months) | Exeter, NH

Medical Billing, Coding, Accounts Receivable for NH Neurospine. Perfoming collections for Workers Compensation accounts. Temporary Position

Instructor Professional Medical Billing and Coding
Joan Bastek
March 2009 – September 2009 (7 months)

Self Contracted Instructor for Post Secondary Education.
Course List:
Medical Terminology, Understanding Health Insurance, CPT and ICD9 Coding, English, Business Mathematics, Microsoft Office, Word and Excel, Medisoft

In her skills section, Joan is highly endorsed for many of the keywords found in medical billing and coding job descriptions:

Most endorsed for...

23	Medical Billing
12	HIPAA
10	Medical Terminology
10	CPT
10	ICD-9
9	Healthcare

For the position *you* desire, make sure you repeat all the essential keywords in your profile, particularly in the summary, skills, and headline.

3. Make sure your LinkedIn profile has a targeted headline. Not only should the headline clearly state your career focus, it's also the most important place to add a keyword or two, because this influences how you appear in search results (and how easily you're found by staffing professionals). You should add keywords that reflect your desired title, strengths, and perhaps industry you want to be in. Consider this headline:

> IT Project Manager at Data Research | 10+ years' experience managing financial software development using Agile methodology

It's jam-packed with keywords ... and tells a story.

Although we saw some more creative headline examples in Chapter 1, when you're job hunting it's more important to be clear and direct. Here are a few more examples that illustrate various experiences and situations:

- *Community Relations and Policy Executive Seeking New Opportunity*. The phrase "Seeking new opportunity" is sometimes searched for by recruiters.

- *Recent UCLA Honors Graduate Seeking Legal Intern Position*

- *Assistant Vice President of Sales at Aspen Automotive Group*. Short and simple works too.

  INSIDER TIP: Don't use terms like "Job Hunting" or "Unemployed" in your headline. These terms aren't searched for, and cast a more negative light on your profile.

How to Address Gaps and other Special Job Seeker Situations

What if you don't have much experience, want to change careers, are re-entering the workforce, or are looking to relocate? Here's how to put your best LinkedIn foot forward for these special situations.

Leverage all relevant experience. *Any* professional experience you have, paid or unpaid, could make up for gaps in your career (for example, if you were a stay-at-home parent or unemployed for a long period of time) or if you don't have much experience in your desired field. Definitely include relevant volunteer work, freelance work, or advising and consulting in your profile. Describe these positions as you would a full-time job. Also include any certification or coursework that relates to skills needed for your desired job.

For example, your summary could say:

> *"I am an account representative with over six years of experience in the retail industry. For the past two years, I have been on hiatus while raising a young family, but am eager to return to a full-time position in sales. I am currently taking classes to achieve certification*

with the National Association of Sales Professionals (NASP)."

Use positive but honest details if you're currently unemployed. Given the recent economic recession, most people are very understanding about periods of unemployment. Don't feel like you have to hide the fact that you're currently unemployed.

When filling out your experience section, one strategy is to use what you do (or want to do) as your title and "Open to New Opportunities" as your current company. Your LinkedIn headline would then look like "Human Resources Manager at Open to New Opportunities."

Two other strategies are to use "Self-Employed" as the company name (if you're doing some freelancing work) or simply leave the company name blank. There's no best way to handle this for everyone, so experiment with one of these examples for a couple of weeks and then maybe try a different one to see what works best for you.

Show you're committed to the new opportunities you're seeking. If you're changing careers, want to get into a certain industry, or are looking to move, use your LinkedIn activity to show your interest in doing so. Join related LinkedIn groups and jump into the discussions (e.g., the Association of Fundraising Professionals or Washington, D.C. Young Professionals). Also update your status to show your enthusiasm for related topics (e.g., the latest donor trends or the best places to see cherry blossoms in D.C.).

If you're transitioning, your profile summary should also reflect the career you want to have (not the one you currently want to switch from). State your interest in transitioning into this new field, emphasize in the experience section the transferrable skills that could apply to your new role, and, again, use keywords from job postings throughout. (Yes, keywords are a prominent theme here!)

How to Find and Apply to Job Listings on LinkedIn

With your profile targeted for job-seeking, it's time to find your potential next job. (Note: If you're concerned about the privacy of your job-searching activities, be assured that when you apply to jobs on LinkedIn, that activity is never broadcast.)

View Recommended Jobs

Click on the Jobs link in the navigation bar to be taken to a page where LinkedIn suggests a number of jobs you might be interested in.

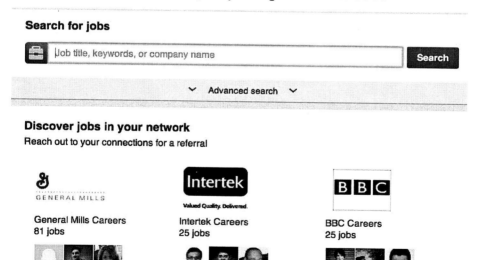

The ones in the "Sponsored" section might not be the best fit (because employers pay to have them up at the top), but the ones beneath that should closely tie into your profile. If they don't, it's a sign you may not be using the right keywords in your profile. (Those keywords again!) Review Chapter 1 as well as the guidelines at the top of this chapter to revise the keywords in your headline and other areas of your profile.

Under the "Jobs you might be interested in" heading is an option to get email alerts of these potential job matches. Click on that link and sign up for daily email alerts (because, as you know, opportunities can disappear quickly!).

On this page, you can view any of the suggested jobs or enter search terms (job title, keywords, or company name) to get a list of many more available jobs.

How to Use LinkedIn's Job Search

After entering a term in the job search form, you'll see a range of available jobs:

Filter your results: You can further refine the results with the options in the sidebar on the left side of the screen:

- Company

- Title

- Location

- Posting date

- Industry

- Salary range (this option is available to paid Job Seeker Premium subscribers, which we'll discuss in more detail later in this guide).

For example, if you don't want to commute any farther than 25 miles from your home, enter your postal code and switch the "Within" field to 25 miles.

Save your search: You don't have to type in your search terms and select filters every time you want to find available jobs. At the top right of the search results, click on "Save search" for easy access on the jobs page. You can save up to ten job searches and also get an email of the search results daily, weekly, or monthly. (Again, opt for daily if finding a job is your top priority.)

View the job listing: Finally, you can view the listings. The job listing provides the ability to apply for the position along with the overview of what the employer is looking for (that's where you'll find the all-important skills and experience section to mine for keywords). You can also save job listings that seem interesting or worth a second look later.

INSIDER TIP: Sort your results by relationship for a greater chance of success. By default, LinkedIn lists jobs by relevance to the search keywords you enter. An even better way to look at the results is to sort by relationship. At the top of the search results, look for "Sort by Relevance" and click the down arrow to switch to "Relationship". This shows you the listings at companies you might have an inside connection to — people who could refer you to the hiring person or tell you more about what it's *really* like to work there.

Find The Most Recently Shared Job Opportunities

Another way to see the latest job postings relevant to your experience is from the LinkedIn home page itself. You can filter the latest updates on the network by jobs listed, to see the freshest opportunities.

- Next to the "All Updates" filter at the top, click the down arrow.

- Select "Jobs" and click Enter.

This will show you the latest job openings from the last day or two.

Jobs ▾

LearnVest, Inc. posted a job you might be interested in:

Senior Editor

Greater New York City Area · Position Scope: LearnVest is seeking a smart, creative, dynamic Senior Editor who will report directly to the Executive Editor during an exciting growth period for the company. We're looking for a...

View Job · More jobs at LearnVest, Inc. · 5h ago

AAA National posted a job you might be interested in:

Freelance Writer (Part-Time)

Orlando, Florida Area · Freelance Writer (Part-Time) North America's largest member service organization is looking for a high-energy business writer and editor with a global perspective to work as a freelancer covering national and...

View Job · More jobs at AAA National · 5h ago

SHOW MORE UPDATES

How to Apply to Jobs on LinkedIn

To apply to a job on LinkedIn, just click the "Apply Now" or "Apply on Company Website" button found on the listing. As with other online job search sites, make sure you follow the job application requirements (résumé format, required information, and so on). Also, when you apply to a job through LinkedIn, your profile will be included with the application, so make sure your profile is updated appropriately.

A week to 10 days after applying to the position, follow up with a recruiter, hiring manager, or interviewer with a polite email — and sprinkle in information from the company research you did above.

How to Access the Hidden Job Market on LinkedIn

LinkedIn's job listings are a valuable resource, but the greatest potential for finding a job through LinkedIn lies elsewhere: In your connections themselves.

70% of job openings are found through networking (rather than job listings), according to the U.S. Bureau of Labor Statistics. Think about that for a second. **A huge number of jobs that are filled are never advertised to the public**, or if they are, they're filled by people who have a connection to the employer. *That's where LinkedIn comes in.*

To tap this hidden job market — opportunities not posted yet — we'll need to do a little networking. Again, if that word makes you groan, don't worry. It's painless, I promise!

How to Network on LinkedIn When You Need a Job

Think of networking as simply reaching out to the people you're connected to on LinkedIn. Send a message to your connections telling them the types of opportunities you're looking for, ask for advice for your job search (people love giving advice!), and ask if they could help keep an eye out for any available positions for you. Remember, as with all messages you send on LinkedIn, it's better to create individual messages rather than a generic blast. Don't forget to add your willingness to be of help to the other person as well.

Another place to find possible job referrers is in LinkedIn groups. Look for job opportunities posted by the group manager and members under the group's Jobs tab. You could also turn fellow group members into direct connections by sending an invitation request. In your message, offer to be a resource for that person.

Update your status frequently on LinkedIn so other members will see you regularly. Show that you're involved in your industry and open to opportunities (e.g., "Heading to the tech music conference in Austin. Hope to network with you there!" or "Just read this interesting study on brain waves and music in *The Atlantic*"). Every three or four weeks, share a message that you're in the market. For instance: "As some of you may already know, I'm looking for new opportunities in business administration. I'd appreciate any referrals you can send my way!"

A LinkedIn Job-Searching Strategy

Here's a plan you can use to more effectively job search with LinkedIn, beyond regularly looking at the job listings:

- **Keep your profile current**. Update it whenever something significant changes or if you need to use more precise keywords for the jobs you're finding.

- **Update your status** at least a couple of times a week, so you stay top-of-mind with your connections.

- Monthly or every few weeks, update your status **mentioning you're seeking new opportunities**.

- **Follow companies you're interested in working for** — especially the ones where many of your connections work.

- **Save job searches** and set up daily alerts to get new listings in your email inbox.

- **Participate in relevant groups, recommend or endorse others**, and **comment on or "like"** your connections' status updates (when appropriate).

- **Post your LinkedIn vanity URL** on your blog or personal website, if you have one, as well as in your email signature and business cards.

- **Try to connect with people offline as well**. LinkedIn should supplement your real-life job-seeking efforts.

There are also a few tools you can use to enhance your job search on LinkedIn. I've gathered them in Chapter 5, which contains power user tips and other resources. For now, let's head to the next chapter to learn how to enhance your career prospects, whether you're currently employed or not.

Chapter 4

How to Use LinkedIn to Advance Your Career

In the last chapter, we looked at the many ways LinkedIn can help you find a job or support your job-seeking efforts. LinkedIn is also a powerful tool even if you're not currently looking for work. The site can help you maintain your job skills, develop a career plan, and stay current in your industry. Let's take a look.

How Using LinkedIn Can Enhance Your Career

I have a confession to make. Once upon a time, I was a lackluster LinkedIn member. My profile was basically a duplicate of my résumé. I rarely interacted with other members. I didn't join any groups.

In other words, I was like many people who are "on" LinkedIn but not seriously using it because the site is seen as more of a job-searching tool.

After learning about all the ways LinkedIn can help professionals in all stages of their careers, I wish I had been using LinkedIn more effectively from the very beginning.

For one thing, just having an updated profile and being active on the network makes you a more attractive employee or career professional. It's like wearing a badge that says "Yes, I care about my career and what I do (and I'm poachable!)."

Also, I think we've all realized by now that no job lasts forever. It's better to be ahead of the curve by being active on LinkedIn and cultivating relationships *before* you need it to find a job.

There's more. LinkedIn is also a gold mine of information about people, companies, and industries. It's growing increasingly more valuable as a career enhancer, with more tools and features being regularly added to the network. Here are some of the best ways you can use LinkedIn for your career right now.

Stay Current in Your Industry

In many fields, keeping abreast of the latest trends is crucial. This means not only knowing the latest news in your industry, it also means monitoring the conversations and "buzz" that help drive your industry forward. LinkedIn has tools that can help.

News on LinkedIn

On LinkedIn's homepage and Interests section, you'll find the latest articles for your industry and interests. Here's what the news page ("LinkedIn Today," under Interests > Influencers > Your News) looks like:

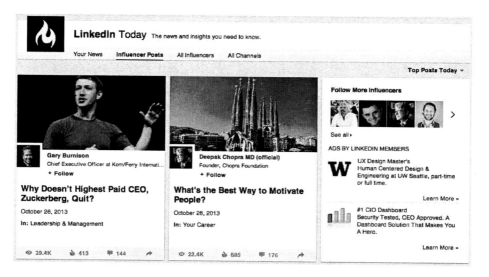

You might be thinking, "I already get my news elsewhere, why would I do that on LinkedIn?"

First, LinkedIn's news feeds come from a variety of sources: top trending articles from around the web (tailored to your preferences under the "All Channels" tab), as well as content shared or recommended by your connections. It could be very useful to keep on top of what your peers are reading and sharing.

You can customize the LinkedIn Today news to follow specific industries or topics and "influencers" (famous people with useful advice). This adds richness to the news feeds, and you might see content here that you otherwise might miss (Influencer Posts, in particular, are exclusive articles written for LinkedIn by industry leaders).

Also, LinkedIn is all about business. You're less likely to find shared videos of dancing babies or articles on giant snail invasions on LinkedIn (unless you work in a related industry, in which case, I would love to meet you!). In other words, you won't find low-value distractions and time-wasters on LinkedIn. That's a good thing when you're in a productivity mindset.

The quality content extends to LinkedIn's mobile apps as well, thanks to LinkedIn's recent purchase of the Pulse newsreading app for mobile devices. This makes it easy to get tailored, professional content on the go through LinkedIn's apps for iOS, Android, and other devices.

Find Out What Others Are Talking About on LinkedIn

Other ways to stay current on what's happening in your industry are to follow specific companies' pages on LinkedIn (as mentioned in the previous chapter) or join relevant groups (as mentioned in Chapter 2). Both of these steps will deliver updates to your email inbox and LinkedIn homepage.

Maintain Relationships and Find People Who Can Help You

By now you might have started adding status updates, endorsing your connections, and jumping into group discussions, as recommended in the last few chapters. These all help you build and maintain your professional identity online — and keep you connected to valuable contacts.

One last networking tip is to find people (in or outside your LinkedIn network) who could offer advice on either your job search, career path, or any other professional matter. Do an advanced search to find them by clicking the "Advanced" link next to the search box.

For example, if you want to find professional photographers on LinkedIn who are close enough to have an in-person informational interview, in the

"Title" field, type "Photographer," and then use the options under "Location" to restrict the results to those near you. Look at their profiles for things you have in common (such as groups), and send a message asking for an informational interview or advice. It could be something like this:

> *"Hi Joe, I saw from your LinkedIn profile that you're a fellow UNC alum and member of the National Professional Photographer's Association group like me. I was hoping we could connect because I really admire your work (your cover on National Geographic last month was stunning) and would like to learn how to become a successful photographer like yourself. I understand how busy you are, but would you be willing to have a brief phone call with me or lunch even to talk about your work and experiences? Thanks so much, Dave."*

Keep in mind, this isn't the time or place to directly ask for a job. Even if your contact is willing to have an informational interview with you, treat it as a knowledge-seeking opportunity (that could later lead to other opportunities).

Chapter 5

LinkedIn Power User Tips and Tricks

In the previous chapters, we explored how the key to using LinkedIn effectively is creating a focused, active presence on the professional network. We've looked at: how to create a strong profile targeted towards your career goals; grow your network and interact with your connections; use LinkedIn to find a job; and take advantage of career-enhancing tools on the service. Finally, let's look at some lesser-known tips and tricks to *really* take your LinkedIn membership to the next level.

How to Send a Message to (Almost) Anyone on LinkedIn for Free

As discussed in Chapter 2, if you want to send a message to someone on LinkedIn who isn't a direct connection, you are supposed to pay for a special LinkedIn service called InMail. While InMails let you send a message to anyone (who hasn't blocked incoming messages), they aren't free.

There is a free workaround, however (but don't tell anyone I told you!). Here's how to do it:

1. Look at the person's profile to see what LinkedIn groups he or she belongs to.

2. Join one of those groups yourself.

3. On the group page, click on the number of members link at the right of the group name.

4. Search the group for the member.

5. Once you've found the member, look for the no-fee "Send message" link below the name.

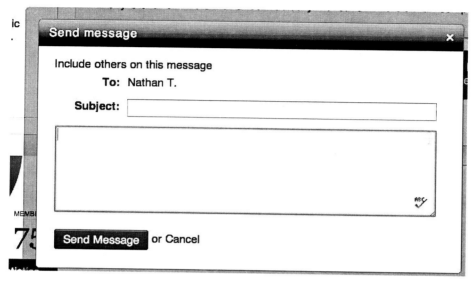

The workaround has a few conditions:

- You're able to see which groups that person belongs to (some people hide profile sections from the public)

- He or she belongs to a group you can join

- The person hasn't disabled the default setting of allowing messages from fellow group members.

Organize Your LinkedIn Connections

All that work building your LinkedIn empire (I mean, network) has a downside: A terribly crowded contacts list. Thankfully, LinkedIn offers a couple of ways to make more sense out of your expanding network list:

LinkedIn Contacts and custom tags.

View Contact History and Stay Connected with LinkedIn Contacts

LinkedIn Contacts is a relatively new feature that allows you to add and see more details about your LinkedIn connections. It integrates with applications and services outside of LinkedIn, including Outlook, Gmail, Yahoo! Mail and Contacts. By syncing services such as these with LinkedIn Contacts, you'll have an all-in-one contact management tool on LinkedIn — one that reminds you of your colleagues' birthdays or new jobs, shows you the last time you were in touch with them, and helps you remember more of their important details.

With LinkedIn Contacts you can visit any of your connections' profile pages and:

- Add personal notes (which your contact will never see), such as a reminder that this person prefers text messages over phone calls or that his name is really Bobby and not Robert (see screenshot below)

- View a history of messages and meetings, including emails and appointments from services you connect to LinkedIn

- Set a reminder to reconnect to the person in a day, week, or month

- Add a tag to add the person to a group of similar contacts (see the section on tags below)

Here's what it looks like:

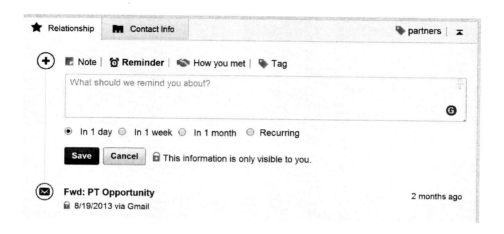

Organize Your Connections with Custom Tags

Tags are keywords or key phrases that group contacts together (for example, "former co-workers," "partners," "graduate school," etc.). To add tags to your contacts:

- Click on Network in the navigation bar and then Contacts to get a list of all your connections.

- Check the box next to the name of each connection you want to edit.

- At the top of the contacts list, click "Tag."

- From the drop-down box, check existing tags to add them to your contact(s) or click the "Add New Tags" link if you want to great a new one.

- You can do this for each individual contact or en masse (e.g., select all your fellow classmates at once to add the same tag to all of them).

FYI, the tags you add to your contacts are for your eyes only.

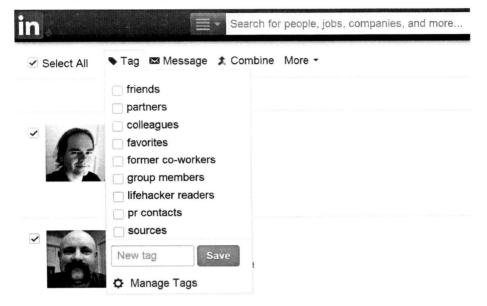

Tweak Your LinkedIn Privacy Settings

As with any online social network, controlling your privacy on LinkedIn is extremely important. Luckily, LinkedIn's account settings let you specify the information you share with specific groups. Click on your profile photo and then Privacy & Settings to review this information.

The main ones you'll want to check here are your:

- **Public Profile**: Click on "Edit your public profile" in the Profile section. This displays how your profile will appear to everyone who visits your profile page (e.g., from a Google search results link).

Uncheck the sections on the right you don't want the world to see.

- **Activity Feed**: Also in the Profile section, click on "Select who can see your activity feed" and change the setting to: just you, just your connections, everyone in your network, or the internet at large. Your activity feed includes all your actions on LinkedIn, from status updates to profile changes and new connections.

- **Email Notification Settings**: In the Communications section, you can set how often LinkedIn sends you email and the kinds of messages you're willing to receive (see screenshot below). For example, in the frequency of emails setting, you can specify you want emails to be sent individually for job suggestions, but network updates only as a weekly email.

- **Privacy Controls**: If you don't want your data shared with third-party applications or advertisers, head to the "Groups, Companies, & Applications" section, and make sure the options for sharing your activity under Privacy Controls are unchecked.

Messages from other members
Invitations, messages, and other communication from LinkedIn members

Invitations to connect	Individual Email ⬍
Invitations to join groups	Weekly Digest Email ⬍
Messages from connections	Individual Email ⬍
InMails, introductions and OpenLink messages	Individual Email ⬍
New connection suggestions	No Email ⬍
Profiles sent to you	Individual Email ⬍
Job suggestions from connections	Individual Email ⬍

[Save changes] [Cancel]

It's really worth going through all of the settings options so you know what you're sharing. They're mostly self-explanatory, and you can fine-tune just how much information you share on the network. Keep in mind, though, that the more you share, the more you might get out of LinkedIn (since this is, after all, a *social* network).

Paid LinkedIn Accounts

So now you've seen the many uses for and features of LinkedIn available with the free, basic account. LinkedIn also offers upgraded, paid subscription accounts for job seekers, sales professionals, recruiters, and others. Let's take a look at what these premium accounts have to offer.

Job Seeker Premium

Job Seeker Premium (not to be confused with LinkedIn Premium, below) starts at $19.95 per month (a bit cheaper if you pay yearly). For this price, you get:

- "Featured applicant" status: Your application moved to the top of the list of applicants for jobs posted on LinkedIn

- A premium "job seeker" badge added to your profile

- The ability to see the names of people who have viewed your profile

- Premium search features, such as a salary range for job listings

- Participation in the OpenLink network, so anyone on LinkedIn can send you a message

- Access to LinkedIn job-seeker groups and online seminars

Of these features, the most valuable one for job seekers is the prominent featured applicant status when you apply to jobs. However, if many people are paying for Job Seeker Premium accounts, they'll *also* be at the top of the list. So I think unless you need these premium benefits, you'll save a lot of money by skipping the paid account and focusing instead on improving your keywords and networking efforts on LinkedIn.

LinkedIn Premium

Similarly, LinkedIn Premium, starting at $19.95 a month (or less if you pay yearly), offers advanced features most useful for only certain types of professionals. LinkedIn Premium includes a number of InMail messages, so you can contact LinkedIn members outside of your network (but we've seen a workaround to that earlier), as well as membership in the OpenLink network, which means anyone on the network can freely contact *you*. OpenLink is like saying, "Hey, I'm here. Go ahead, ask me anything."

Premium membership also gives you access to more search filters, more profiles per search, and more saved search results. And you can see the full list of people who have looked at your profile (great for solving the stalker curiosity problem, but probably not very useful overall.)

Generally, I don't think the paid plans are worth it unless you rely on LinkedIn for business development or your job depends on using LinkedIn to reach out to numerous people regularly.

In any case, hopefully the strategies and tips in the previous chapters will make the professional network more useful for you, whether you want to grow your existing career or find a new one. In addition, be sure to visit the official *LinkedIn In 30 Minutes* website, which contains bonus materials, videos, and other resources that will help you get more out of LinkedIn. The URL is linkedin.in30minutes.com.

A Personal Message From The Author, And A Request

Thank you for purchasing *Linked In 30 Minutes*! LinkedIn has been a valuable tool in my own career, and I wrote this book so you can also take your career to the next level as quickly and as easily as possible.

After reading the book, please do me a favor and take a minute to rate and review *LinkedIn In 30 Minutes*. You can do so via these sites:

- **Amazon product page for *LinkedIn In 30 Minutes***

- **Apple iBookstore page for *LinkedIn In 30 Minutes***

- **Barnes & Noble product page for *LinkedIn In 30 Minutes***

I'd very much appreciate your honest thoughts about the tips and suggestions in *LinkedIn In 30 Minutes*. Your reviews will also let other potential readers know what to expect.

Thanks for reading, and congratulations on taking this next step in your career!

Melanie Pinola

P.S.: If you are interested in browsing other *In 30 Minutes*® guides, please visit in30minutes.com to see the available titles. To be notified of future releases, you can sign up for our free e-newsletter at in30minutes.com/newsletter, or like our Facebook page at facebook.com/in30minutes.

About the Author

Melanie Pinola is a writer who specializes in technology and productivity. She has over a dozen years' experience in content development for both the web and traditional media.

Pinola began her career at a marketing agency in Long Island, New York, where she designed marketing materials and developed communication strategies for clients of all kinds, from startups to Fortune 500 companies.

Today, she regularly writes for Lifehacker, ITworld, and About.com's Mobile Office Technology sites. Her work also appears on *Popular Mechanics* and other publications.

In 2011, *New York Times* columnist Virginia Heffernan called Pinola "the Poppy Cannon of our time." Pinola thinks this means she's been called a low-key, everyday, and super-efficient kind of geek, but she's not sure. In any case, that's how Pinola approaches LinkedIn and networking in general: low-key, everyday, and super-efficient.

You can find Pinola on Twitter at @melaniepinola and, of course, LinkedIn at linkedin.com/in/melaniepinola. (Don't forget to personalize your connection invitation!).

Credits

Thanks to **Ian Lamont** for all his work editing and publishing this guide, **Jodie Naze** for graciously connecting me to Ian, and fellow writer-in-the-trenches **Kevin Purdy** for connecting me to Jodie in the first place. Networking works (often when you least expect it to and don't realize it's happening)!

My husband, Rob Pinola, patiently read five times as many words in drafts as you see here in this guide, my parents, Felipe and Ma.Ester Uy, encouraged me to continue beyond the introduction, and my daughter, Elise, forced me to write as fast as I could to get it done in time for our next playdate.

The cover was produced by Steve Sauer of Single Fin design. Greg Cusack was the copy editor.

Bonus: Introduction To Twitter In 30 Minutes

(The following chapter is the introduction to Twitter In 30 Minutes: How to connect with interesting people, write great tweets, and find information that's relevant to you. *The guide, by author Ian Lamont, is available as an ebook, PDF, and paperback via twitter.in30minutes.com)*

One January afternoon when I was at work, I saw a remarkable event unfold on Twitter.

It was around 3:30 p.m., and I was sitting at my computer. A few people I followed on Twitter suddenly began sending out short text messages (called "tweets") about a plane crash. The plane had apparently gone down in New York City, right in the Hudson River. New Yorkers in nearby buildings had seen the crash, or saw a plane in the river, and were sharing scraps of information in the short, 140-character text messages that Twitter allows.

I checked CNN and Google News. There were no official reports, but people on the ground were reporting a disaster. What was going on?

Then I saw someone share a remarkable photograph on Twitter:

The photo showed survivors standing on the wing, or stepping into a boat. The tweet that accompanied the photo said:

> *There's a plane in the Hudson. I'm on the ferry going to pick up the people. Crazy.*

I did not know Janis Krums, the person who took the photo or sent out that message on Twitter. But the information he posted on Twitter indicated that many passengers were alive, and were in the process of being rescued. Krums' friends shared the message, which was shared again to thousands of other people. Considering there was no official report or news account of what was happening, it was reassuring to see Krums' tweet.

The story of US Airways Flight 1549 is now well-known, thanks to the quick thinking and professionalism of Capt. Chesley B. "Sully" Sullenberger and his crew. More than 150 people were on the plane when it ran into a flock of geese and crash-landed. It could have been a tragedy. Yet every passenger survived.

But the crash-landing and rescue was important for another reason: It showed that Twitter was more than just a collection of fleeting observations about everyday life. Twitter could connect people to events, information and each other in ways that had never been experienced before.

What Is Twitter?

Twitter is a free tool that can connect you with interesting people, events and information. Twitter is available online at twitter.com, or as a free app that can be installed on a mobile phone or tablet. Millions of people all over the world consider Twitter to be as important to their daily communications routines as checking their email, sending text messages or catching up with friends on Facebook.

How do people use Twitter? I use it to keep up to date with current events, and to let people know about my business and whereabouts. Other people use it in different ways. Here are a few real examples:

- **Abby** (@AbbyLeighTaylor) is an Oklahoma native now living in Nashville. She loves using Twitter to connect with people who share her musical interests and Mexican food.

- **Fiona** (@EmeraldFaerie), a jewelry designer based in London, uses Twitter to show off her latest creations, and let customers know where they can be purchased.

- **The New York Public Library** (@nypl) tweets about 10 times per day about library programs, author appearances, photographs from its archives, and even job openings.

- **Steven** (@IamStevenT) is none other than Steven Tyler, the hard-rock singer and TV personality. On Twitter, he talks about his tour schedule and television appearances, and also uses Twitter to connect with his fans.

- **Chayce** (@BehnkeChayce) is a young father and sports fanatic (Cleveland Browns, Buffalo Bills and Ohio State). He uses Twitter to talk about sports with other fans and ask questions related to his favorite teams.

- **Mark** (@mcuban) is a famous entrepreneur who uses Twitter to promote his business interests and basketball team, the Dallas Mavericks. He also answers questions from people who have seen him on TV, have read his book or follow his blog.

- **James** (@JamesBondTheDog) is the self-proclaimed "international hound dog of mystery." Like many parody accounts on Twitter, the focus is on humor ("Apple, you showed a squirrel at your press conference. You have my attention."). Many of James' followers are pet owners who have created Twitter accounts for their dogs.

As you can see from these examples, there are all kinds of people, organizations and interests represented on Twitter. Further, they use Twitter for varied purposes — connecting with like-minded people, promoting their businesses or causes, and having fun.

However, if you are new to Twitter, it can be bewildering. There are strange symbols and unfamiliar conventions. It may not be apparent how Twitter can help you connect with people or start conversations.

This guide is intended to help you get your bearings and teach you how to get the most out of Twitter. *Twitter In 30 Minutes* concentrates on core skills and use cases that a beginner should understand. In the next 30 minutes, you'll learn how to do everything from setting up and personalizing your account online or using a mobile phone (Chapter 2), to finding interesting people and topics to follow (Chapter 3). There's a chapter that discusses how to tweet (Chapter 4). You'll even learn a few tricks, ranging from hashtags to retweeting (Chapter 5).

What Can Twitter Do For You?

At its heart, Twitter lets you do three things:

1. **Broadcast to the world what you are doing, what you are thinking and who you are with.** The broadcasts are short messages called "tweets" that contain no more than 140 characters of text. It's also possible to add a photograph or a link to a news story as well. While anyone can see these tweets, the messages are most likely to be noticed by people who "follow" you on Twitter (more about that later).

2. **Monitor what other people are saying and doing.** Millions of ordinary people — as well as companies, schools, sports teams, charities, politicians and superstars — broadcast their own messages to the world. You can choose to follow the accounts of people you like or who you think are interesting. When you follow someone, you will be able to see their recent tweets. Some may even follow you back, to see what you have to say!

3. **Learn about the world.** Because people all over the world use Twitter to describe what they are doing, how they are feeling and what they are seeing, Twitter is a window into events, opinions, and information. Want to know what other people think about the latest episode of your favorite TV show or sports team? Want to see photographs taken at a concert, beach or political rally? Twitter can let you do that. The flow of information is sometimes rough, but it

grants an unfiltered view of the world, often before "official" sources of news weigh in.

We only have 30 minutes, so let's get started with Twitter!

To read the rest of this guide, visit twitter.in30minutes.com.

Bonus: Introduction To Google Drive & Docs In 30 Minutes

(The following bonus chapter is the introduction to Google Drive & Docs In 30 Minutes, *by author Ian Lamont. If you're interested in downloading the ebook or purchasing the paperback, please visit the guide's official website, googledrive.in30minutes.com.)*

Thanks for your interest in *Google Drive & Docs In 30 Minutes*. I wrote this unofficial user guide to help people get up to speed with Google Drive, a remarkable (and free) online office suite that includes a word processor (Docs), spreadsheet program (Sheets), and slideshow tool (Slides). The guide also covers the storage features of Google Drive.

How do people use Google Drive and Docs? There are many possible uses. Consider these examples:

- **A harried product manager needs to continue work on an important proposal over the weekend**. In the past, she would have dug around in her purse to look for an old USB drive she uses for transferring files. Or, she might have emailed herself an attachment to open at home. Instead, she saves the Word document and an Excel spreadsheet to Google Drive at the office. Later that evening, on her home PC, she opens her Google Drive folder to access the Excel file. All of her saves are updated to Google Drive. When she returns to work the following Monday, the updated data can be viewed on her workstation.

- **The organizer of a family reunion wants to survey 34 cousins** about attendance, lodging preferences, and potluck dinner preparation (always a challenge — the Nebraska branch of the family won't eat corn or Garbanzo beans). He emails everyone a link to a Web Form created in Google Drive. The answers are automatically transferred to Google Sheets, where he can see the responses and tally the results.

- **A small business consultant is helping the owner of Slappy's Canadian Diner** ("We Put The Canadian Back In Bacon") prepare a slideshow for potential franchisees in Ohio. The consultant and Slappy collaborate using Google Slides, which lets them remotely access the deck and add text, images, and other elements. The consultant shares a link to the slideshow with her consulting partner, so he can periodically review it on a Web browser and check for problems. Later, Slappy meets his potential franchise operators at a hotel in Cleveland, and uses Slides to give them his pitch.

- **An elementary school faculty uses Google Docs to collaborate on lesson plans**. Each teacher accesses the same document from their homes or classrooms. Updates are instantly reflected, even when two teachers are simultaneously accessing the same document. Their principal (known as "Skinner" behind his back) is impressed by how quickly the faculty completes the plans, and how well the curriculums are integrated.

- At the same school, **the 5th-grade teachers ask their students to submit homework using Docs**. The teachers add corrections and notes, which the students can access at any time via a Web browser. It's much more efficient than emailing attachments around, and the students don't need to bug their parents to buy expensive word-processing programs.

Many people try Google Docs because it's free (Google Drive is, too, if you store less than five gigabytes of data). Microsoft Office can cost hundreds of dollars. While Google Docs is not as sophisticated, it handles the basics very well. Docs also offers a slew of powerful online features that are unmatched by Office or Apple's iWork suite, including:

- The ability to review the history of a specific document, and revert to an earlier version.

- Simple Web forms and online surveys that can be produced without programming skills or website hosting arrangements.

- Collaboration features that let users work on the same document in real time.

- Offline file storage that can be synced to multiple computers.

- Automatic notification of the release date of Brad Pitt's next movie.

I'm just kidding about the last item. But Google Drive and Docs really can do those other things, and without the help of your company's IT department or the pimply teenager from down the street. These features are built right into the software, and are ready to use as soon as you've signed up.

Even though the myriad features of Google Drive may seem overwhelming, this guide makes it easy to get started. Google *Drive & Docs In 30 Minutes* is written in plain English, with lots of step-by-step instructions, screenshots and tips. Videos and other resources are available on the companion website to this book, googledrive.in30minutes.com. You'll get up to speed in no time.

We've only got a half-hour, so let's get started with Google Drive and Docs!

If you're interested in learning more about this title, or buying the ebook or paperback, visit the official website located at googledrive.in30minutes.com.

More In 30 Minutes Guides

Readers are raving about *In 30 Minutes*® guides:

Dropbox In 30 Minutes:

> "This was truly a 30-minute tutorial and I have mastered the basics without bugging my 20-year-old son! Yahoo!"

Google Drive & Docs In 30 Minutes:

> "I've been using Google Docs for a while now and have been encouraging my teacher colleagues to do so as well to facilitate collaboration. It has become my go-to text book to help new users understand quickly. If you're new to Google Drive or Google

Documents, this will help you."

Excel Basics In 30 Minutes:

"I have used Excel in the past in only a very limited fashion. I learned from your book how to use formulas, make charts, and sort. I will have to play with the charts a little more - there are so many options that it feels like a whole other program! The "ninja" autofill function is awesome!"

All guides are available as paperbacks and in ebook formats, including downloads for the Kindle, iPad, and Nook. They can also be downloaded as full-color PDFs. Visit In30Minutes.com to learn more about the guides, and access purchase links, free videos, blog posts, and other resources!